# Thinking Outside
# the Lunchbox

# Thinking Outside the Lunchbox

## RAINIE SHIN

iUniverse, Inc.
Bloomington

# Thinking Outside the Lunchbox

*iUniverse books may be ordered through booksellers or by contacting:*

*iUniverse*
*1663 Liberty Drive*
*Bloomington, IN 47403*
*www.iuniverse.com*
*1-800-Authors (1-800-288-4677)*

*ISBN: 978-1-4620-4599-0 (sc)*
*ISBN: 978-1-4620-4600-3 (ebk)*

*Printed in the United States of America*

*iUniverse rev. date: 08/05/2011*

# Contents

## Sides and Salads

## Fish and Shellfish

# Pasta

# Introduction

Are you tired of having the same lunch meal everyday? Do you think you deserve more than just a plain sandwich for lunch after hours of hard work? Is cooking one of your hobbies?? If you answer yes to any of these questions, then this recipe book is for you.

Imagine having a tough day. You've been working hard since the beginning of the day but the workload just doesn't seem to get done. Finally it's lunch break, time for you to get back those energies you've lost. So you open your lunchbox and what do you see? A grilled cheese sandwich! Very disappointing isn't it? You need something more appetizing than just a sandwich. Of course there's always the convenience of cafeteria foods and fast food restaurants are everywhere. But then again, why spent your money on something you're not sure will satisfy your hunger when you can make your favorite lunch meal more appetizing? Here's an idea, how about turning that grilled cheese sandwich from plain into something fancy?

With recipes that you can mix and much for a perfect lunch combo, thinking outside the lunchbox will be your everyday companion that will introduce you to new recipes as well as some alternatives to transform an ordinary dish into something extra ordinary.

# The Things You Need

# To Know

# Friendly Reminder

1. Make sure that your hands are clean before cooking and always rinse vegetables and fruits with cold water. Herbs like parsley and cilantro tend to be very sandy so make sure you change the water a few times when rinsing it.
2. Cooking is a form of art and a recipe is just a guide to help you get started. Just because it is given to you, doesn't mean you have to follow every single thing that is written. You have to keep this statement in mind, especially when you're using an oven because the temperature varies from one oven to another. When it comes to the recipe itself, you can always make it your own by adding few more ingredients or use the same ingredients but different method of cooking.

# Cooking Temperature

|         | Rare             | Medium                      | Well Done                   |
|---------|------------------|-----------------------------|-----------------------------|
| **Beef**    | 130ºF (54ºC)  | 140º-145ºF (60º-63ºC)       | 160ºF (71ºC)                |
| **Pork**    |                  | 150º-155ºF (66º-68ºC)       | 165º-170ºF (74º-77ºC)       |
| **Chicken** |                  |                             | 180ºF (82ºC)                |

# Sandwiches

# and

# Sandwich Alternatives

# Grilled Cheese French toast

## Ingredients:

- 8 slices white bread
- 4 slices cheddar cheese
- ½ cup milk
- ¼ tsp cinnamon
- 2 tsp butter
- 2 eggs

## Preparation:

1. Melt butter in a skillet over medium high heat. Meanwhile, whisk together eggs, milk and cinnamon. Dip bread slices in the mixture one at a time.
2. Place bread into skillet, add a slice of cheese and place another slice of bread on top. Grill until browned on one side and flip over. Continue grilling until cheese is melted.

# Grilled Caprese Sandwich

## Ingredients:

- 8 slices white bread
- 2 pieces bocconcini cheese (sliced)
- 2 large tomatoes (sliced)
- ¼ cup basil (chiffonade)
- ¼ cup balsamic vinegar
- 3 tbsp olive oil
- 2 tsp butter
- Salt and pepper (to taste)

## Preparation:

1. Pre-heat oven to 300 degrees F. Place tomatoes and basil into a baking dish. Whisk together balsamic vinegar, olive oil, salt and pepper and pour mixture over tomatoes and toss everything together. Bake for about 15 minutes. Set aside.
2. Melt butter in skillet over medium heat. Place a slice of bread into skillet. Add 2 slices of baked tomatoes and 2 slices of bocconcini on top and place another slice of bread. Grill until golden brown and flip over to brown the other side.

# Baked BLT

## Ingredients:

- 8 Ice berg lettuce leaves
- 8 slices Canadian bacon (diced)
- 1 large tomato (diced)
- 2 Eggs
- 1 cup flour
- 1 cup breadcrumbs

## Preparation:

1. Heat oil in a skillet over medium heat and cook bacon and tomatoes for 2 minutes.
2. Distribute mixture to the lettuce leaves evenly. Fold bottom of each lettuce over filling, then fold in ends and roll into tight cylinder and secure with a toothpick.
3. Beat eggs. Coat each wrap with flour, dip into egg and coat with breadcrumbs. Place breaded wraps in a baking dish and bake in a preheated oven (350 degrees F) for 15 minutes or until golden brown. Remove toothpicks.

# Turkey Lettuce Wrap

## Ingredients:

- 8 boston lettuce leaves
- ½ pound ground turkey
- 1 tsp cumin
- 1 medium onion (brunoise)
- 1 tsp garlic powder
- Tomato concasseé
- ½ tsp chili flakes (optional)
- ¼ cup worcestershire sauce
- ¼ cup sesame oil
- ¼ cup soy sauce
- 1 tsp lemon juice
- 1 tsp butter
- Salt and pepper to taste

## Preparation:

1. In a small bowl, whisk together sesame oil, soy sauce and lemon juice. Set aside.
2. Heat butter in a skillet over medium-high heat. Sweat onion and add cumin, garlic powder, chili flakes and tomato concasseé. Cook for a few minutes. Add ground turkey, worcestershire sauce, salt, pepper and continue cooking until turkey is well browned.
3. Divide turkey mixture evenly to 8 lettuce leaves. Drizzle with soy sauce mixture and wrap lettuce around the fillings.

# Taco Burger

## Ingredients:

- 8 pcs tortilla wraps
- 1 lb ground beef
- 10 slices bacon (chopped)
- 1 cup shredded cheddar cheese
- 2 cloves garlic (minced)
- 1 medium size onion (finely chopped)
- 1 tsp fresh chopped mint
- Salt and pepper to taste
- Roasted Corn and jalapeno salsa (p11)
- 2/3 head romaine lettuce (broken into bite size pieces)

## Preparations:

1. Cook bacon in a skillet without adding butter or any fat of some sort. Remove the bacon and reserve the fat.
2. Sweat the onion using the fat rendered from the bacon.
3. In a large bowl, Mix together ground beef, cooked bacon, onion, mint. Shape mixture into 4 patties.
4. Grill patties in a pre-heated grill (medium heat) for about 5 minutes on each side or until well done.
5. Divide romaine lettuce and cheese evenly to 4 tortilla wraps. Place one patty on each wrap, add a tablespoon of salsa and place another wrap on top. Grill taco burgers for about 1 minute on each side.

# Roasted Corn and Jalapeno Salsa

## Ingredients:

- 1 cob corn
- 1 sprig mint (chiffonade)
- ½ cup tomato concassé
- 1 lime (juice and zest)
- Salt pepper

## Preparation:

Grill corn in a pre-heated grill (medium high heat). Cut corn kernels from the cob and place it in a bowl. Add tomato concassé, mint and zest and juice of 1 lime. Season with salt and pepper.

# Meatball Fajita

## Ingredients:

- 1 lb Ground beef
- 1 medium size onion (brunoise)
- 1 tsp garlic purée
- 1 carrot (grated)
- 1 sprig parsley (chopped)
- 1 tbsp garam masala (mixture of ground cumin, coriander, cardamom, clove, cinnamon and pepper)
- Salt and pepper (to taste)
- ¼ cup beef stock
- 1 cup tomato sauce
- 1 sprig cilantro (chopped)
- 1 medium size red onion (julienne)
- 2 cups mozzarella cheese(grated)
- 1 tbsp olive oil
- 4 pitas (cut in half)

## Preparations:

1. In a large bowl, mix the first 7 ingredients together. Scoop about a tablespoon of the mixture and form into a ball. Do the same with the rest of the mixture.
2. Heat olive oil in a skillet over medium heat and brown meatballs. Add cilantro, tomato sauce, beef stock and simmer for 10-15 minutes.
3. Place 1/8 of meatballs in pocket of each pita and top with red onion and cheese.

# Choco-Bananna Nut Sandwich

## Ingredients:

- 8 slices whole wheat bread
- 3 Bananas (sliced)
- Nutella spread
- ½ cup ground almonds

## Preparation:

Toast breads. Spread nutella to each bread slice and add ground almonds. Distribute banana slices to 4 breads evenly and top with another piece of bread.

# Chicken Caesar Sandwich

## Ingredients:

- 1 ciabatta bread loaf
- ½ head romaine lettuce (torn)
- ½ cup plain yogurt
- 1 tsp lemon juice
- 1 tsp mustard powder
- 1 tsp garlic powder
- 2 tsp olive oil
- 2 chicken breasts
- 1 cup parmesan cheese (shaved)
- 1 medium sized red onion (julienne)
- Salt and pepper (to taste)

## Preparation:

1. In a bowl, mix together yogurt, lemon juice, mustard powder, garlic powder, olive oil, parmesan cheese, salt and pepper.
2. Meanwhile, preheat grill over medium heat and grill chicken breast until well done and cut into strips.
3. Cut the bread in half (lengthwise). Spread each slice with a small amount of yogurt mixture. Use the rest of the mixture to coat grilled chicken breast. Arrange lettuce and red onion on one slice, add chicken breast and place the other slice of bread on top. Cut the bread in half.

# Chili on a Bun

## Ingredients:

- 4 hamburger buns
- 15 oz kidney beans
- 1 lb ground beef
- 1 green bell pepper (diced)
- 1 red bell pepper(diced)
- 1 cup raisins
- 1 large tomato (diced)
- 1 tbsp tomato paste
- ¼ cup beef stock
- 1 tsp paprika
- 1 tsp chili flakes
- 1 tsp hot pepper sauce
- 2 cups cheddar cheese (grated)
- 1 medium size onion (brunoise)
- 1 clove garlic (minced)
- 1 tbsp olive oil
- Salt and pepper (to taste)

## Preparation:

1. Heat the oil in a large pot over medium heat. Sweat onion for a few minutes and add garlic, and bell peppers. Stir in ground beef, paprika, chili flakes, tomato paste and continue cooking for 5 minutes.

2. Add beans, tomatoes, hot sauce and beef stock. Season with salt and pepper and cover Simmer for about 45 minutes, stirring occasionally.
3. Add raisins and simmer for another 10 minutes.
4. Distribute chili to the buns evenly and top with cheddar cheese.

# Meat and Poultry

# Inside Out Cordon Blue

## Ingredients:

- 4 skinless, boneless chicken breast (pound)
- 4 slices ham
- 4 slices swiss cheese
- Pineapple juice
- 1 sprig fresh rosemary (chopped)
- 1 tsp paprika
- 1 cup flour
- ¼ cup butter
- Salt and pepper to taste

## Preparation:

1. Pre-heat oven to 350 degrees F (175 degrees C).
2. In a bowl, mix together the flour, rosemary, paprika, salt and pepper.
3. Brush each piece of chicken on both sides with pineapple juice and sprinkle with salt and pepper.
4. Place 1 slice of ham and 1 slice of Swiss cheese on top of each breast. Roll up each breast, secure with a toothpick and coat with the flour mixture.
5. Heat butter in an oven-safe skillet and cook the chicken until all the sides are brown. Remove toothpicks and cover the skillet with foil. Put it in the oven to finish cooking. (about 20 minutes)

# Spicy Chicken Kebab

## Ingredients:

- 4 skinless, boneless chicken breast (cut into chunks)
- 1 can pineapple chunks (juice reserved)
- 1 tablespoon lime juice
- 1 teaspoon garlic powder
- 1/2 teaspoon turmeric powder
- 1/2 teaspoon ground black pepper
- 1/2 teaspoon chili pepper
- 1/4 cup pineapple juice
- 3/4 cup sodium soy sauce
- 1 red onion, cut into cubes (about the same size of the chicken)
- Cooking oil
- 8 pcs wooden skewer (soak in cold water)

## Preparation:

1. In a bowl, mix together lime juice, pineapple juice, garlic powder, turmeric powder, ground pepper, chili pepper and soy sauce.
2. Place chicken and red onion in a large glass bowl and pour in soy sauce marinade. Cover with plastic wrap and put in the fridge for at least two hours.
3. Pre-heat grill to medium heat. Thread chicken onto skewers, alternating with red onion and pineapple chunks. Lightly oil the grill. Brush chicken skewers with marinade and grill for about 8 minutes on each side or until chicken is cooked through.

# Lemon Thyme Chicken

## Ingredients:

- 4 skinless chicken breast
- 6 sprigs fresh thyme
- 2 cloves garlic (purée)
- 1 lemon (zest and juice)
- ¼ cup olive oil
- Salt and pepper (to taste)

## Preparation:

1. In a large bowl, whisk together lemon, thyme, garlic, olive oil, salt and pepper. Marinate chicken for at least an hour.
2. Preheat grill to medium heat, lightly oil and grill chicken for about 10 minutes on each side or until fully cooked. Let it rest for 10 minutes and cut in bias if desired.

# Mushroom Stuffed Beef Tenderloin

## Ingredients:

- 1 3 lb beef tenderloin
- 1 ½ cup crimini mushroom (chopped)
- 6 pcs bacon (diced)
- 1 medium onion (brunoise)
- 1 clove garlic (minced)
- 1 cup beef stock
- 2 tbsp butter
- 2 tbsp flour vegetable oil
- Salt
- Pepper

## Preparation:

1. Simmer beef stock in a sauce pan. Meanwhile, cook bacon in a skillet. Set aside and reserve fat.
2. Using bacon rendered fat, sauté onion and add mushrooms and garlic. Season with salt and pepper.
3. Trim the silverskin and excess fat from the tenderloin and cut it lengthwise (almost, but not completely in half). Open it and pound to ½ inch thickness. Place mushroom stuffing on top of the beef and roll it. Secure with butcher's twine. Pre-heat oven to 375 degrees F (190 degrees C). Heat vegetable oil in a roasting pan over medium high heat. Add tenderloin and sear until all sides are brown. Finish

cooking in the oven for about 30 minutes or until it reached your desired doneness.

4. Melt butter in a sauce pan. Add flour and whisk constantly until it reaches a mahogany brown color. Add beef stock little by little and add bacon. Cook until the sauce reaches the consistency of gravy.

5. Pour the sauce on top of the tenderloin.

# Picadillo

## Ingredients:

- 1 lb ground beef
- 1 potato (peeled, macédoine)
- 1 carrot (peeled, macédoine)
- 1 red bell pepper (macédoine)
- 1 egg (hard boiled, sliced)
- 1 cup tomato sauce
- 1 cup beef stock
- 1 medium size onion (brunoise)
- 2 garlic cloves (minced)
- 1 bay leaf
- 1 tbsp soy sauce
- Olive oil
- Salt and pepper (to taste)

## Preparation:

1. Heat oil in a large saucepan over medium heat and sweat onion until transparent. Add garlic and cook for 1 minute. Stir in ground beef and cook until brown.
2. Pour in stock, tomato sauce, and soy sauce, add bay leaf and bring to a boil. Season with salt and pepper and add potato and carrots. Simmer for about 10 minutes or until vegetables are tender.
3. Adjust seasoning and garnish with hard boiled egg on top.

# Pork Stew

## Ingredients:

- 1 lb pork tenderloin (cut into ½ inch cubes)
- 1 red pepper (cut into cubes)
- 1 green pepper (cut into cubes)
- 1 yellow pepper (cut into cubes)
- 1 medium size onion (cut into cubes)
- 1 clove minced garlic
- ¼ cup all-purpose flour
- 2 tbsp butter
- 2 tbsp tomato paste
- 2 tbsp paprika
- 12 oz beer
- 2 cups beef stock
- Spice bag (5 sprigs fresh thyme, 2 bay leaf, peppercorn) salt vegetable oil

## Preparation:

1. Coat pork tenderloin with flour (shake off excess fat). Heat butter in a skillet over medium-high heat. Add pork and cook until browned on each side. Set aside.
2. Heat vegetable oil in a large pot. Sweat onion for a few minutes and add tomato paste and paprika. Cook until onion is tender.
3. Add pork, bell peppers, garlic, spice bag, beer, stock and salt and bring to a boil. Reduce heat, cover and cook for about an hour, stirring occasionally.

# Sides and Salads

# Hawaiian Rice

## Ingredients:

- 1 ½ cup water
- 1 cup uncooked rice
- 1/4 cup green bell pepper (brunoise)
- 1/4 cup red bell pepper (brunoise)
- ½ cup diced ham (cooked)
- ½ cup sundried tomatoes (sliced)
- 1 tin pineapple chunks
- ½ cup pineapple juice
- ½ bunch green onion (chopped)
- Vegetable oil
- Salt to taste

## Preparation:

1. Heat vegetable oil in a saucepan. Sweat onions and bell peppers until soft.
2. Add rice, salt and pepper and sauté for a few seconds. Add water and pineapple juice. Cover and turn the heat to medium low. Cook until rice is tender and has absorbed all the liquid.
3. When the rice is cooked, stir in the rest of the ingredients.

# Curried Fried Rice

## Ingredients:

- 4 cups left over rice
- 1 small size red pepper (julienne)
- 1 small size yellow pepper (julienne)
- 1 medium onion (brunoise)
- ½ tsp garlic puree
- ½ tsp ginger puree
- 1 tablespoon Curry powder
- ½ tbsp cumin
- Vegetable oil
- Salt and pepper to taste
- ¼ bunch fresh parsley (chopped)

## Preparation:

1. Sweat onion and bell peppers in vegetable oil until soft.
2. Add rice, garlic and ginger puree, cumin and curry powder. Season with salt and pepper and cook for about 5 to 10 minutes. Add chopped parsley on top.

# Stuffed Rice Balls

## Ingredients:

- 2 cups glutinous white rice (uncooked)
- 4 cups water
- 2 cloves garlic (minced)
- 100 g button mushroom (sliced)
- ½ cup saseme seeds (toasted)
- 1 tbsp sesame oil
- ½ tsp lemon juice
- 4 tbsp soy sauce
- 2 tbsp vinegar
- Salt and pepper (to taste)
- Olive oil

## Preparation:

1. Rinse the rice until the water runs clear. Combine with water and a pinch of salt in a medium saucepan. Bring to a boil, then reduce the heat to low, cover and cook for 20 minutes.
2. Meanwhile, heat olive oil in a skillet over medium heat. Add mushrooms and cook for 2 minutes. Add garlic, vinegar, 2 tbsp soy sauce, pepper and cook for another 2 minutes without stirring. After 2 minutes, stir and continue cooking until the liquid evaporates. Set aside.

3. Wet your hand with cold water and pick up a handful of rice. Form into a ball and firmly press it. Place about a teaspoon of sautéed mushroom into the center and reshape into a ball. Roll the balls in the sesame seeds until they are completely coated.
4. For the dipping sauce, mix together lemon juice, sesame oil and 2 tbsp soy sauce.

# Udon Noodle Stir Fry

## Ingredients:

- 2 7-oz packets of fresh udon noodles
- 1 carrot (julienne)
- 1 zucchini (julienne)
- 1 medium size onion (julienne)
- 1 bunch spinach (washed)
- 1 lb top sirloin grilling steak (cut into thin strips)
- 100 g bean sprouts
- ½ tsp worcestershire sauce
- ¼ cup soy sauce
- 1 tsp garlic (purée)
- 1 tbsp sugar
- 3 tbsp sesame oil
- Vegetable oil
- Salt pepper

## Preparation:

1. Marinate sirloin in worcestershire sauce, 1 tbsp soy sauce, 1 tbsp sesame oil and garlic for at least 30 minutes.
2. In a wok or a large skillet, drizzle vegetable oil and stir fry carrots zucchini and bean sprouts. Set aside.

3. Sauté onion. Add sirloin and 1 tbsp of the marinade and cook for a few minutes. Add udon noodles, sugar and the rest of the soy sauce and cook for a few minutes, stirring every once in a while. Add pepper and more salt if necessary. Stir in spinach in the last minute and turn the heat off. Add stir fried vegetables and the rest of the sesame oil and stir. Sprinkle sesame seeds on top.

# Spaghetti Squash

## Ingredients:

- 1 Spaghetti squash (halved lengthwise and seeded)
- 2 sprigs basil (chiffonade)
- 1 Canned tuna
- 1 cup tomato sauce
- 1 cup olives (cut into 3)
- 1 medium onion (brunoise)
- 1 clove garlic (minced)
- Salt and pepper (to taste)
- 1 tsp garlic powder
- 1 tsp ground rosemary
- Olive oil

## Preparation:

1. Preheat oven to 350 degrees F. Sprinkle squash with salt, pepper, nutmeg, garlic powder and rosemary and drizzle with olive oil. Place it in a baking dish with a bit of water and bake for about 45 minutes or until tender.
2. Meanwhile, heat oil in a skillet over medium high heat and sauté onion until tender. Add garlic; sauté for a few minutes and add tuna and tomato sauce. Season with salt and pepper and cook for about 5 minutes.
3. Using a fork, or a spoon to scoop the inside of the squash and place in a bowl. Toss with sauce, basil and olives.

# Apple mash

## Ingredients:

- 4 medium russet potatoes (peeled and cut into cubes)
- 2 golden delicious apples (peeled and cut into cubes)
- ¼ cup butter (room temperature)
- 1 tsp apple juice
- ¼ tsp cinnamon
- ¼ tsp nutmeg
- 1 sprig parsley (chopped) salt and pepper (to taste)

## Preparation:

1. Place potatoes, apples and salt in a saucepan and cover with water. Bring to a boil; cover and cook until tender.
2. Drain the potatoes and apples. Add butter, apple juice, cinnamon, nutmeg, parsley and pepper and mash until smooth. Add more salt if necessary.

# Apple and Fennel Slaw

## Ingredients:

- 1 granny smith apple (cored and thinly sliced)
- 2 fuji apples (cored and thinly sliced)
- 1 fennel (thinly sliced)
- 1 medium size red onion (sliced)
- Few sprigs chopped dill (optional)
- 1 lemon (juice and zest)
- 1 tablespoon maple syrup
- 3 tablespoons olive oil
- Salt and pepper (to taste)

## Preparation:

In a small bowl, whisk together lemon juice, maple syrup and olive oil. Mix the rest of the ingredients together in a different bowl and toss with the dressing. Season with salt and pepper.

# Fennel Salad

## Ingredients:

- 1 fennel (slice)
- 1 carrot (grated)
- 1 green mango (julienne)
- 1 sprig cilantro (finely chopped)
- 1 lemon (zest and juice)
- 2 tbsp olive oil
- Salt and pepper (to taste)
- 1 tbsp honey

## Preparation:

1. In a large bowl, mix together fennel, carrot, green mango and cilantro.
2. In another bowl, whisk together lemon juice and zest, olive oil, honey, salt and pepper.
3. Pour dressing over fennel mixture and toss everything together.

# Frisée and Calamari Salad

## Ingredients:

- ½ lb frisée
- 1 ½ lb squid ring
- 1 medium size red onion (sliced into rings)
- 1 egg
- 2 cups all-purpose flour
- 2/3 cup milk
- 2 tsp paprika
- Salt and pepper (to taste)
- 3 tbsp rice wine vinegar
- Vegetable oil (for frying)

## Preparation:

1. Heat deep fryer to 375 degrees F. Meanwhile, whisk together egg, milk, flour, paprika, 1 tsp salt and 1 tsp pepper.
2. Dip squid rings into batter and deep fry until golden brown.
3. In a large-size bowl, mix together frisée, red onion and rice wine vinegar. Add fried squid rings and toss everything together. Add salt and pepper if necessary.

# Vermicelli Salad

## Ingredients:

- 1 (8 ounce) package dried rice noodles
- 2 sprigs parsley (finely chopped)
- 2 sprigs cilantro (finely chopped)
- 1 Limes (zest and juice)
- 2 cups cherry tomatoes (halved)
- Mint (chiffonade)
- ¼ cup olive oil
- Salt and pepper (to taste)

## Preparation:

1. Bring a large pot of salted water to a boil. Add rice noodles and cook for 5-12 minutes or until noodles are soft. Drain and rinse noodles with cold water to keep them from sticking. Set aside.
2. Whisk together lime juice and zest, olive oil, salt and pepper. Pour mixture to the noodles and add parsley, cilantro, mint and tomatoes. Add more lime juice if necessary.

# Saffron Infused Couscous

## Ingredients:

- 1 cup couscous
- 1 ½ cup water
- A pinch of Saffron
- 1 cucumber (brunoise)
- 1 cup diced tomatoes
- 1 lemon (juice and zest)
- 1 tbsp butter
- 2 tbsp olive oil
- 1 tsp honey
- Salt and pepper (to taste)

## Preparation:

1. In a saucepan, bring water, saffron and ½ tablespoon butter to boil. As soon as it boils, stir in couscous. Cover and remove pan from heat. Let stand for 5 minutes. With a fork, fluff couscous and let it cool.
2. In a large bowl, mix together couscous, tomatoes and cucumber. In another bowl, whisk together honey, olive oil, lemon juice, salt and pepper.
3. Pour dressing over the couscous mixture and stir. Add more salt if necessary.

# Hawaiian Couscous

## Ingredients:

- 1 cup water
- 1 cup couscous
- 1/4 cup green bell pepper (brunoise)
- 1/4 cup red bell pepper (brunoise)
- ½ cup sundried tomatoes (sliced)
- 1 tin pineapple chunks (juice reserved)
- ½ bunch green onion (chopped)
- I tablespoon lemon juice
- 2 1/2 tablespoon olive oil
- 1 teaspoon maple syrup
- Salt to taste

## Preparation:

1. In saucepan, bring water, ½ tablespoon olive oil and ½ cup pineapple juice to boil. As soon as it boils, stir in couscous. Cover and remove pan from heat. Let stand for 5 minutes. With a fork, fluff couscous and let it cool.
2. In a large bowl, mix together couscous, bell peppers, sundried tomatoes, pineapple and green onion.
3. In another bowl, whisk together maple syrup, 2 tablespoon olive oil, lemon juice, 4 tbsp pineapple juice, salt and pepper.
4. Pour dressing over the couscous mixture and stir. Add more salt if necessary.

# Fruit Medley

## Ingredients:

- 1 red delicious apple
- Orange (segmented)
- 1 ripe mango
- 2 sprigs fresh mint (chopped)
- 2 tbsp honey
- ½ Lemon (juice only)
- 3 bananas (sliced)

## Preparation:

Cut apple and mango into cubes. Place all ingredients in a bowl with the exception of honey. Melt honey in a small skillet and pour into the fruit mixture. Toss everything together.

# Chickpea Salad

## Ingredients:

- 1 can (15 oz) chickpeas (drained)
- 2 sprigs fresh mint (chiffonade)
- 1 cup cherry tomatoes (halves)
- 2 tbsp balsamic vinegar
- 3 tbsp olive oil
- Salt and pepper (to taste)

## Preparation:

1. In a small bowl, whisk together balsamic vinegar, olive oil, salt and pepper.
2. Place the rest of the ingredients in a bowl and toss together with the dressing.

# Arugula Salad

## Ingredients:

- 6 oz arugula
- 1 fuji apple (cored and sliced)
- 1 medium size red onion (julienne)
- 1 tbsp apple juice
- 2 tbsp balsamic vinegar
- ¼ cup sesame oil
- 1 tsp sesame seeds
- Salt and pepper (to taste)

## Preparation:

1. In a medium size bowl, whisk together balsamic vinegar, apple juice, sesame oil, salt and pepper.
2. Place arugula, apple and red onion in another bowl and toss it with the dressing. Sprinkle sesame seeds on top.

# Broccoli salad

## Ingredients:

- 4 cups broccoli florets
- 1 red delicious apple (cut into cubes)
- 2 tbsp apple sider vinegar
- 1 Lemon (juice and zest)
- 2 tbsp honey
- 1 tbsp Olive oil
- 1 medium size red onion (chopped)
- ¼ cup Raisins
- 2/3 cup Mayonnaise
- ¼ cup walnuts (roughly chopped)

## Preparation:

1. Boil a pot of salted water and blanch broccoli for about minutes.
2. In a bowl, whisk together apple sider, lemon juice and zest, honey, olive oil, mayonnaise, salt and pepper.
3. In another bowl, mix together broccoli, apple, red onion, raisins and walnuts. Pour dressing into the mixture and stir.

# Fish and Shellfish

# Thyme Roasted Shrimp

## Ingredients:

- 1 ½ lb jumbo shrimps (peeled and deveined)
- 6 sprigs fresh thyme
- 1 lemon (zest and juice)
- 2 tbsp balsamic vinegar
- ½ cup olive oil
- Salt
- Pepper

## Preparation:

1. In a large bowl, whisk together lemon zest and juice, balsamic vinegar, ½ cup olive oil and salt and pepper. Marinate shrimps for at least 30 minutes.
2. Pre-heat oven to 400 degrees F. Pour the rest of the oil into a baking dish. Add thyme and bake for about 10 minutes.
3. Add shrimps and marinade to the dish, toss everything together and bake for another 10 minutes or until shrimps are firm.

# Fish Balls

## Ingredients:

- 2 cups flaked whitefish (cooked)
- ½ cup dill (chopped)
- 1 tsp onion powder
- 1 egg
- Salt and pepper (to taste)
- ¼ cup cilantro (chopped)
- 1 tbsp cornstarch
- 1 tbsp brown sugar
- 3 tbsp soy sauce
- 2 tbsp vinegar

## Preparation:

1. Put the first four ingredients together in a food processor and process until the all ingredients are mix evenly. Place in a bowl, add cilantro, salt, pepper and mix using your hand. Refrigerate mixture until it is firm and sticky.
2. Form mixture into small balls. Boil water in a saucepan. Drop balls into the water, remove, and then sauté in oil until brown.
3. To make sauce; Combine soy sauce, vinegar, cornstarch and sugar in a saucepan and simmer until it thickens a bit.

# Spicy Tuna Cake

## Ingredients:

- 2 cans tuna (drained)
- 1 large potato (peeled and quartered)
- 1 small onion (brunoise)
- 1 tbsp chives (chopped)
- 1 egg
- 1 tablespoon dry breadcrumbs, or as needed
- ½ tsp cayenne pepper
- ½ tsp hot paprika salt and pepper (to taste) olive oil

## Preparation:

1. Place potato in a pot and cover with salted water. Cover and bring to a boil. Cook for about 20 minutes or until tender. Drain well, place in a bowl and mash with a potato masher.
2. Whisk the egg and add to the mashed potato. Add the rest of the ingredients and mix thoroughly. Divide mixture into 8 equal portions and form into patties.
3. Heat oil in a skillet over medium heat and fry patties until golden brown on each side.

# Stuffed Calamari

## Ingredients:

- 8 large squids
- 1 cup quinoa
- 2 cups water
- 1 cucumber (brunoise)
- 1 red bell pepper (brunoise)
- 1 lime (juice and zest)
- ½ lemon
- 1 cup cilantro (chopped)
- 1 tsp garlic powder
- ½ cup flour
- 1 tbsp smoked paprika
- Salt and pepper (to taste)
- Olive oil

## Preparation:

1. In a saucepan bring water to a boil. Add quinoa and a pinch of salt. Reduce heat to low, cover and simmer for 15 minutes. Fluff with a fork. Let it cool for a dew minutes.
2. Meanwhile, mix together red pepper, cucumber, lime (juice and zest) cilantro, garlic powder, salt, pepper and a drizzle of olive oil. Toss in quinoa and set aside.
3. Stuffed each squid with quinoa mixture and secure with a toothpick.

4.  In a medium bowl, mix together flour, paprika, salt and pepper and use it to coat each squid.
5.  Heat olive oil in a cast-iron pan. Cook calamari for about 3-4 minutes or until golden brown, turning occasionally. Remove toothpick and squish half a lemon on top.

# Shrimp Frittata

## Ingredients:

- 6 large eggs
- ¾ lb small shrimp (peeled and deveined)
- ½ cup chopped onion
- ½ cup diced tomatoes
- ½ lemon (juice only)
- 1 sprig fresh rosemary (chopped)
- 1 clove garlic (minced)
- 1 ½ tsp butter
- Salt and pepper (to taste)

## Preparation:

1. Whisk egg in a bowl, add salt and pepper. Set aside.
2. Heat butter in a skillet over medium heat. Sweat onion for one minute; add tomatoes, garlic and cook for another 2 minutes. Add shrimp, rosemary, lemon and cook for a few more minutes (until shrimps turned pink). Turn the heat off. Add sautéed shrimp to the beaten egg.
3. Lightly spray an 8-inch baking dish with oil and pour in egg mixture. Bake in a 375 degrees F preheated oven for about 30 minutes or until set.

# Baked Salmon with Mango Salsa

## Ingredients:

- 4 salmon steaks
- ½ cup soy sauce
- ½ lemon (juice and zest)
- 1 tsp garlic powder
- ½ chili flakes

## Preparation:

1. In a large bowl, whisk together soy sauce, lemon (juice and zest), garlic powder and chili flakes. Add the salmon steaks and put in the fridge for at least an hour, turning occasionally.
2. Preheat oven to 375 degrees F. Place salmon in a baking dish (with the marinade), cover with foil and bake for about 30 minutes or until fully cook.
3. Garnish with spicy mango salsa (p47) on top.

# Spicy Mango Salsa

## Ingredients:

- 1 ripe mango (julienne, peeled and seed discarded)
- 1 red bell pepper
- 1 jalapeno (finely chopped)
- 1 sprig fresh cilantro (chopped)
- 1 lime (juice and zest)
- Salt and pepper (to taste)
- 1 tsp olive oil

## Preparation:

1. Roast pepper, peel and cut into julienne.
2. Mix all ingredients together and use as a garnish for baked salmon or you can even add it to meatball fajita (p)

# Sautéed Mussels in Oyster Sauce

## Ingredients:

- 5 lb mussels (cleaned and debearded)
- 2 cloves garlic (minced)
- ¼ cup ginger ale
- 1 tsp chili flakes
- 2 tbsp fermented black beans
- 1 tsp oyster sauce
- 2 scallions (chopped)

## Preparation:

1. Heat oil in a wok or skillet over high heat. Add garlic, and black beans and sauté for a few seconds.
2. Add mussels and cook for 1 minute. Add oyster sauce, ginger ale and chili flakes. Cover and cook until the shells are completely open. Garnish with the chopped scallions on top

# Pasta

# Paella Pasta

## Ingredients:

- 1 pck penne pasta
- ½ lb mussels (scrubbed, debearded and steamed)
- ½ lb medium shrimp (peeled and deveined)
- 2 skinless chicken breast (cubed)
- ½ lb squid rings
- 2 garlic cloves (minced)
- 1 red bell pepper (brunoise)
- 1 medium size onion (brunoise)
- ½ bunch parsley (chopped)
- 1 cup tomato juice
- ½ cup chicken or fish stock
- 1 tsp chili flakes
- 1 tsp paprika
- Salt and pepper (to taste)
- Olive oil

## Preparation:

1. Boil salted water in a large pot and cook pasta according to package. Drain and drizzle with olive oil to avoid pasta from sticking together.
2. Meanwhile, heat oil in a large skillet over medium high heat. Sauté onion, red pepper and garlic. Add chicken and cook for about 10 minutes, stirring occasionally. Add squid rings and cook for another 3 minutes. Add paprika, chili flakes, stock,

tomato juice, salt, pepper and simmer until sauce thickens a bit. Add shrimp and continue cooking for 2 minutes. If sauce gets to thick, add a few tablespoons of water.

3. Add pasta to the sauce and cook for another minute. Decorate with mussels and parsley on top.

# Sweet and Sour Chicken Fettuccine

## Ingredients:

- 1 pck fettuccine
- 4 skinless chicken breast (cubed)
- 2 cups crushed tomatoes
- ¼ cup chicken stock
- 1 sprig fresh basil (chiffonade)
- ½ lemon (juice only)
- 2 tbsp honey
- 2 cloves garlic (minced)
- 1 medium size onion (brunoise) vegetable oil salt and pepper to taste

## Preparation:

1. Bring a large pot of salted water to boil and cook fettuccine for about 8 minutes or until al dente. Drain and drizzle with olive oil.
2. Meanwhile, sauté onion in olive oil. Add garlic and tomatoes and cook for 3 minutes. Add chicken and cook for another 10 minutes. Add lemon, honey, stock, salt, pepper and bring to a simmer. Cook until sauce has thickened a bit.
3. Add pasta to the sauce and cook for 1 minute. Garnish with fresh basil on top.

# Bacon Aioli Penne

## Ingredients:

- 1 pck penne pasta
- 5 slices bacon (chopped)
- 8 cloves garlic (thinly sliced)
- 1 sprig fresh thyme (chopped)
- 1 egg yolk
- ½ parmesan cheese
- Vegetable oil
- Salt and pepper (to taste)

## Preparation:

1. Bring a pot of salted water to boil and cook according to package direction.
2. In a medium size bowl, whisk together egg and cheese.
3. Cook bacon in a skillet over medium heat. Remove bacon and reserve fat. Using the bacon fat, sauté garlic and chili flakes for about 2 minutes or until it sizzles. Set aside.
4. Heat butter in a skillet over medium heat. Add pasta, egg mixture, bacon garlic, thyme, salt, pepper and cook for about 2 minutes.

# Carbonara

## Ingredients:

- 1 pck angel hair pasta
- 2 skinless chicken breast (cut into strips)
- 2 slices ham (cut into small pieces)
- ½ cup cream of mushroom
- ½ cup heavy cream
- 2 garlic cloves (minced)
- 1 medium size onion (brunoise)
- ½ bunch parsley (chopped)
- Salt and pepper (to taste)

## Preparation:

1. Bring a pot of salted water to a boil and cook pasta according to package direction. Drain and drizzle with olive oil.
2. Heat butter in a skillet over medium heat. Sauté onion and garlic. Add chicken and cook for 10 minutes, stirring occasionally. Add ham, cream of mushroom, heavy cream, salt, pepper and simmer until the sauce thickens a bit.
3. Add pasta to the sauce and cook for one more minute. Add chopped parsley on top.

# Bacon Mac and Cheese

## Ingredients:

- 8 oz elbow macaroni (uncooked)
- 6 slices bacon (diced)
- 1 sprig parsley (chopped)
- ¾ cup mayonnaise
- 1 cup parmesan cheese
- ¼ cup cheddar cheese

## Preparation:

1. Bring a pot of salted water to boil. Add macaroni and cook according to package direction. Drain and set aside.
2. Cook bacon in a skillet over medium heat. Discard fat.
3. In a large bowl, mix together cooked macaroni, bacon, mayonnaise, parsley, pepper and parmesan cheese.
4. Transfer into a baking dish; sprinkle cheddar cheese on top and bake in a 350 degrees preheated oven for 20-30 minutes.

# Tomato Mac and Cheese

## Ingredients:

- ½ pck fussili pasta
- 1 ½ cup crushed tomatoes
- 1 sprig basil (chiffonade)
- 1 cup parmesan cheese
- ¾ cup mozzarella cheese
- Salt and pepper (to taste)

## Preparation:

1. Bring a pot of salted water to boil. Cook pasta according to package direction; drain.
2. In a large bowl, mix all ingredients together with the exception of mozzarella cheese. Transfer into a baking dish and sprinkle mozzarella cheese on top.
3. Bake in a 350 degrees F preheated oven for 20-30 minutes.